Personal
Communicating
AND
RACIAL EQUITY

Kendall Hunt
publishing company

John Stewart, Ph.D.

Kendall Hunt
publishing company

www.kendallhunt.com
Send all inquiries to:
4050 Westmark Drive
Dubuque, IA 52004-1840

Copyright © 2016 by John Stewart, Ph.D.

ISBN 978-1-4652-9847-8

Kendall Hunt Publishing Company has the exclusive rights to reproduce this work,
to prepare derivative works from this work, to publicly distribute this work,
to publicly perform this work and to publicly display this work.

All rights reserved. No part of this publication may be reproduced,
stored in a retrieval system, or transmitted, in any form or by any
means, electronic, mechanical, photocopying, recording, or otherwise,
without the prior written permission of the copyright owner.

Printed in the United States of America

CONTENTS

CHAPTER 6

CHAPTER 7

CHAPTER 8

CHAPTER 9

CHAPTER 10

CHAPTER 11

ACKNOWLEDGMENTS

I've been engaged in interpersonal communication teaching, training, and research since the 1970s, and I appreciate all the students, colleagues, workshop participants, and trainees who have helped me refine and test the personal relationship-building skills that are summarized in Chapters 2 through 6 of this book. I'm especially grateful to Allen Clark and Helen Felton, Maurice Friedman, Milt Thomas, Karen Zediker, Lyall Crawford, Faith Smith, Laura Black, Jody Nyquist, Bob Arundale, Gerry Philipsen, Kim Pearce, and John Shotter.

My schooling in the 1950s and 1960s included some great teachers and textbooks, but I learned little about inclusion, equity, or racial history of the United States. I was taught that Native Americans had been put on reservations, and I could drive through some of them near my hometown. We studied the Civil War, of course, and a little about slavery which, we were taught, was eliminated by Lincoln's Emancipation Proclamation. We learned that Chinese workers were exploited by railroad builders; the KKK hated Catholics, Jews, and non-Whites; and that ethnic groups were demonized in both World Wars.

I learned almost nothing about how the idea of "race," without any scientific basis, has been used in the United States for 400 years to disempower and brutalize Native Americans, Irish, Italians, Poles, Jews, Chinese, Japanese, Latino/

as, and especially Blacks. I learned nothing about the 3/5th clause in the Constitution, the argument for calling U.S. Western expansion genocide, southern lynchings as a government-approved system of terror, the horrors of slavery and Jim Crow, Denmark Vesey's Rebellion, the struggle to integrate the U.S. Armed Forces, the blatant racism in the administration of the G.I. Bill, homophobia, sexism, or the other violent realities that would help prompt the civil rights movement.

These parts of my education came later in life from people culturally different from me, especially African Americans and LGBTQ people, whom I'm grateful to count as friends. These are my equity teachers, and I could not have written this without especially their help.

In Seattle, my thanks go to Esther and Don Mumford, Connie and Mike Moorehead, Mary and Ben Morales, Zola Mumford, Rudy Hill, and Vivian Caver who helped show me how to be an ally of Blacks. Bill Burgua and John Paul Olafson, Ralph Carskadden, Mason Brock, Cindy King, Aimee Carillo-Rowe, Allen Fowler, Dean Tedder, and George Diestel (Fresno) helped me learn about LGBTQ worlds.

In Iowa and Wisconsin, I've profited from the writings of Glenn E. Singleton, Debbie Irving, bell hooks, Ta-Nehishi Coates, Mitchell Hammer, Milton Bennett, Ruby K. Payne, Michelle Alexander, David Pilgrim, and several others. But I've learned the most from local friends and teachers, Henry Grubb, Tiye Sherrod, Andre Lessears, Alice Oleson, Anderson Sainci, Lauren Alleyne, Al Felice, Mishreen Ellis, Quincy Bufkin, Malcom Stewart, Anthony Allen, Kelly Larson, Taj Suleyman, Monica Grubb, Lynn Sutton, Farris Muhammad, and Miquel Jackson. My deep thanks to each of you.

chapter one

ANDERSON'S CHALLENGE

Photo © 2016 Nicole M. Story

[
"Racism hurts the city's economy and violates social justice!
How can our community be more inclusive?"
]

This question draws together about fifty of us from places like IBM, Mercy Medical, Hillcrest Family Services, the YMCA, the Multicultural Family Center, Prudential, and John Deere, who make up a network of local organizations. Anderson Sainci and I have just sat through a ninety-minute meeting on the results of the Community Equity Profile that the network completed to better understand how diverse groups experience life here. We researched how accessible our city's economic, housing, education, health, transportation, safety, and arts & culture resources are for all populations. We now have data to show where and how it's difficult for marginalized citizens to take advantage of these resources. It's clear that discrimination infects us just like it contaminates every U.S. town and city.

Most of us in the room are frustrated. The study confirms what we either feared or knew already: Racial equity is a problem here. But how do you attack discrimination rooted in systemic racism—White-dominated lending, educational, law-enforcement, voting, and health systems; landlords who've learned not to trust newcomers who don't look like them; and decades of entrenched prejudices fueled by polarizing politicians?

Nationwide, the problems of systemic racism are impossible to ignore. They're illustrated by the Chicago police shooting of Laquan McDonald; Michael Brown's killing in Ferguson, Missouri; and the racially skewed application of drug laws documented in *The New Jim Crow*.[1] They're documented in Ta-Nehisi Coates's acclaimed *Between the World and Me*.[2] They show themselves in the bombing of the African Methodist Episcopal Church in Charleston, and the Department of Justice's $335 million fine of Countrywide Finance for charging Blacks and Hispanics higher mortgage rates and fees even when they qualified for better loans. Systemic racism continues in the atrocities committed since I wrote these words.

PERSONAL COMMUNICATING AND RACIAL EQUITY

Many racially privileged people—most often Whites—are usually respectful and want to be inclusive, but, whether we like it or not, we are still parts of these systems, and it's impossible to change systemic racism by yourself.

And we don't have to do it alone. Systems are made up of individuals who can support each other. As efforts in many cities show, together Whites and other ethnic groups can create ways to dismantle racist practices. We just need to know how to do it effectively.

"The people and organizations in this room need to work more together," Anderson and I hear in the meeting. "Cultural differences don't usually create problems when you know the people personally." "It's harder to stereotype somebody you know well." "The key is to build relationships." "What we need to do better is to build relationships."

The meeting ends without reaching any conclusions. I glumly exit with Anderson, and we commiserate about what we just experienced. "People can learn how to develop relationships if they work at it," I complain. "But everybody wants an instant fix. They don't want to invest the effort it takes to get better at something this important. They just want sound-bites."

Anderson asks what I mean, and I give him a short version of Chapters 2 to 6 of this book. "OK," he says. "Maybe you can help people learn to develop relationships. But exactly how does that improve inclusiveness? Exactly how can better relationships build racial equity?"

I think of what Martin Luther King, Jr. said:

> People fail to get along with each other because they fear each other. They fear each other because they don't know each other. They don't know each other because they have not properly communicated with each other.[3]

Over the next weeks, I reflect on Anderson's challenge and King's response. I realize that, although there are well-tested ways to help people develop person-to-person communicating, the news events I mentioned show that racial equity is among the biggest problems facing the U.S. population today, and so far nobody's applied what's known about building personal relationships to help fix this gnawing problem.

That's what this book does. It's short, because, even though its topics deserve hundreds of pages of historical description, research support, and especially concrete examples, if they were all here, very few people would read it.

So instead, this manual shows you, one small step at a time, in brief chapters and simple language, how to help your communicating be *as personal as possible* (Chapters 2–6), and then it demonstrates how personal relationships can foster racial equity (Chapters 7–11). You might think of it as step-by-step IKEA assembly instructions, but in words rather than pictures, and designed, not to help you build a bookcase, but to enhance your multicultural competence.

chapter two

TAKING IN AND GIVING OUT

© Monkey Business Images/Shutterstock.com

Let's start with the two basic ways we all communicate—taking in and giving out. Every time we communicate—online, in meetings, on the phone, even when we avoid bumping into people while crossing the street—we are both taking in and giving out communication cues.

TAKING IN

"Taking in" is a term for the internal, nonverbal, and verbal ways we come to understand. "Taking in" includes the expectations and agendas we bring to an exchange and any stereotypes that are operating (e.g., "I only have a couple of minutes," "He's probably not going to say much to an old White guy," "I hope she doesn't bring up her divorce again").

"Taking in" also includes your facial expression, body orientation, eye contact, head nods, and what you do with your tablet or smartphone. When crossing the street, subtle glances and body angles inform people how to avoid each other. In a face-to-face situation, do you look away when the topic gets intense? This might shorten what she says. Do you encourage him by leaning forward, nodding, and making noises that show you're listening ("Uh-huh," "Oh?" "Yeah"). Studies show that the mere presence of a phone, even if it's turned off, affects how much people talk.[4] Small things are noticed.

The verbal parts of "taking in" include the questions you ask (e.g., open versus closed questions), whether you paraphrase what you hear, and whether you offer word-based following behaviors like adding an example from your own experience that makes his point. You can also encourage the other person to "Say more," or you can repeat a key word with a questioning inflection in your voice. For example, in response to the previous sentence you might say, "Repeat?" And I would likely say something like, "Yeah, when you say it back he'll elaborate on what he's saying." This is how your mirror response ("Repeat?") can help you understand.

To put it simply, "taking in" is another term for full and complete listening. I use this less-common term so you don't think of just being quiet so the other person can talk.

GIVING OUT

"Giving out" is the other half of your communicating, including the topics you talk about, what you disclose about yourself, and the verbal and nonverbal ways you hold up your end of the conversation. Do you focus on a topic that's linked to what the other person is saying or one that leads in a completely different direction? Research shows that topic relevance is one of the main contributors to a successful conversation.[5] Is your topic appropriate for the situation or too personal for the group you're in? Are you appropriately open about your own experience with this topic and your best ideas about what to do next? Topics work best when they're relevant and appropriate.

Nonverbally, does your body fit what you're saying, or do you shout, "I'm not MAD!!" or insist "I'm fine" when you feel and look lousy? Is your talk animated enough to show that you care about what you're saying? Are you looking at the other person(s) while you're talking, or looking over their shoulders or at your feet?

Verbally, do you own the opinions and feelings you express, for example, by using I-statements? An I-statement begins with the word "I," uses a present-tense verb, and is concrete and specific, such as "I'm worried that half of the people here are undocumented," "I think that meeting was a waste of Jerry and Lauren's time," or "I'm encouraged by what she said." Do you relate stories that make your point memorably? Do you use metaphors to do the same thing, like "I feel caught between a rock and a hard place" or "Being Black on this campus is like having a second full-time job"?

When you want to smooth your interactions with people who are different from you by helping to make your communicating as personal as possible, you need to pay attention to both taking in and giving out processes, which mean how you *listen* (expectations, nonverbal parts, verbal parts) and how you *talk* (topic, nonverbal, verbal).

chapter three
USING ALL YOUR BRAIN POWER

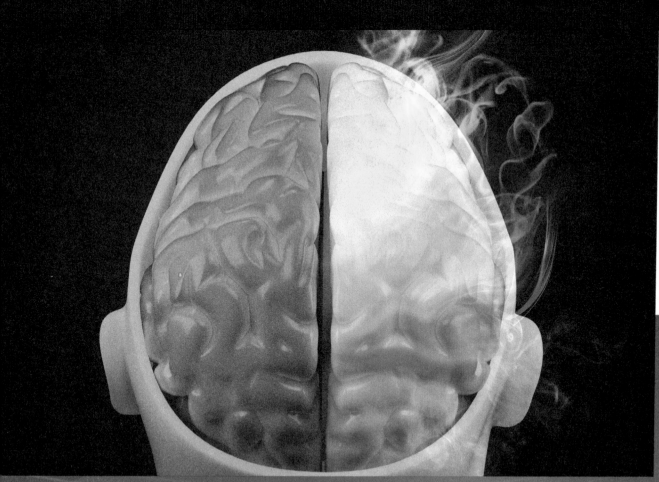

© Mopic/Shutterstock.com

Exactly what do you take in and give out?

Try this: While you're in a room with several other people, pick up your smart-phone or sit down at your tablet or laptop and connect with somebody you mainly know on social media. Notice how it feels to read this person's status update and scan a photo. Then put down your phone or tablet, stand up, move away from your chair, and greet somebody face to face. Shake this person's hand, give him or her a brief hug, or do whatever's normal for this relationship. Chat with this person for a few minutes. Notice how this exchange feels.

How would you describe the differences between these two experiences? When I try this experiment with a group of people and ask this question, I usually hear something like, "The second one's more personal." Some people feel more comfortable with the distance and control they get when connecting digitally, but they still agree that face-to-face contact is more personal.

This response makes a distinction familiar enough to most of us that we don't even think about it. There's a sliding scale between "impersonal" and "personal" that can describe every experience we have. Social media connections aren't completely "impersonal," but they're a lot less "personal" than meeting face to face.

It turns out that this impersonal–personal distinction names something really important about how our human brain empowers each of us to understand every part of our lives.

Since the 1950s, brain scientists have known that we can relate to what we see, hear, taste, smell, and touch in two very different ways. These ways have been called "left-brain" and "right-brain," and some executive trainers have oversim-plified them into "left = logic, right = emotion."

This notion of a simple split between the logical and emotional parts of our brain is misleading and out of date. In its place, today's neurobiologists explain that, while we are hard-wired to understand what's around us in two ways, they're not just "logical" versus "emotional." We can understand in analytic, objective, literal, and generalizing ways, and we can also understand in ways that are holistic rather than analytic, engaged rather than objective, metaphoric more than literal, and that recognize uniqueness rather than just membership in a group. One important brain scientist calls the first of these "impersonal" and the second "personal."[6]

OUR BRAIN'S WAYS OF UNDERSTANDING

Impersonal	Personal
Analytic	Holistic
Objective	Engaged
Literal	Metaphoric
Grouping	Recognizing Uniqueness

PERSONAL UNDERSTANDING

This difference is hugely important. Every one of us has the capacity to look at a landscape, for example, and to *analyze* or divide the scene into parts—fields, roads, buildings, and hills—and to *group* the different features, for example into natural versus human made. Each of us also has the capacity to notice the *uniquely* complex colors of the *whole* scene in this light, or the *unique* way the shapes of farm buildings fit into their surroundings. You might also notice how the scene looks like a painting you've seen (*metaphor*). The first way of understanding works well if you're an engineer or builder, and the second if you're a photographer or painter.

What do you see?

Personal understanding can be easiest to understand with music. Remember the last time you really got into a song? If you're over 40, it might have been a classical piece, a show tune, or a song by the Beatles or Aretha Franklin. If you're younger, it might have been by Taylor Swift, Ariana Grande, Usher, or Kanye West. The music filled your world. Your body moved to it; you might have closed your eyes and moved your head and arms as you *felt* its rhythms and melody. For a time, you were lifted out of wherever you were. You were transformed. The music *happened to you.*

This was the personal part of your brain operating. You may not have this experience very often, but that's because the culture around us pushes us in impersonal directions. It can happen much more often, and not only with music, painting, or poetry. You can also relate to people this way.

This personal way of relating to people probably happened to you as a child, and you may not recall it distinctly. All you remember is that it was a special time with your mom, dad, or grandparent at the beach, at bedtime, on a mountain or desert trail, at church, or during a holiday. This kind of experience probably happened, too, when you realized you were in love. You were so focused on your partner that you had little concept of time; his or her presence overshadowed everything else; and you felt like you were glowing inside. Poets and songwriters try to describe these moments.

A milder version of personal understanding can happen even in your business life. When you're in a meeting with six or seven others, you might notice that a rival is in the meeting and seethe with resentment—this is *engaged* (personal), the opposite of *objective* (impersonal) understanding. Or, when you notice who's present, you might feel lifted up by how much you appreciate and enjoy working with these people. You might be excited enough (engaged) that you greet several with smiles, touches, and eager enthusiasm. You might feel that this is exactly the right group to answer the question the meeting was called to address (uniqueness).

These differences in how your brain operates can lead to very different responses. Impersonal understanding usually leads to impersonal communicating— separating yourself from others, keeping a straight face, not saying much. Personal understanding leads in the opposite direction—smiling and greeting others, some openness, paying attention to the people who are marginalized in this meeting, personal comments and stories, brief touches while you're talking.

DANGERS OF IMPERSONAL UNDERSTANDING

Both of these ways our brain enables us to relate to the world are important, and, as I noted, they're often mixed together. Unavoidably, though, cultural forces push people to favor one or the other. The cultural forces that shape the worlds of many tribal people lead them to engage personally with their surroundings. Apache, Sioux, Algonquin, and Aboriginal descriptions of land-scapes and humans are usually holistic and metaphoric, and many tribal people notice uniquenesses that most urban Whites miss. On the other hand, most of us are not in tribal cultures, and we're affected strongly by the cultural forces of smartphones, tablets, and laptops that lead us to engage much more impersonally with both what's on our screens and the people around us.

Our non-screen lives are also pushed in impersonal directions by ten-lane high-ways, large lectures, robo-calls, mass mailings, and stereotypes about "immigrants," "Muslims," and "the 1%." All these experiences make it easy to depersonalize and objectify others. These cultural forces have shaped us to the point where some of the personal capacities of our brains have actually gotten weaker. As *Forbes* puts it,

> It seems the younger generations are deeply hungry for meaningful face-to-face interactions . . . . We've deemed these generations to be the most connected, but they may, in fact, be the most *disconnected*.[7]

MIT professor Sherry Turkle's fifteen years of research leads her to worry,

> These days, the first generation of children that grew up with smart-phones is about to or has recently graduated from college. Intelligent and creative, they are at the beginning of their careers, but employers report that they come to work with unexpected phobias and anxieties. They don't know how to begin and end conversations. They have a hard time with eye contact. They say that talking on the telephone makes them anxious. It is worth asking a hard question: Are we unintentionally depriving our children of tools they need at the very moment they need them? Are we depriving them of skills that are crucial to friendship, creativity, love, and work?[8]

In another book, Turkle explains,

> ...we are changed as technology offers us substitutes for connecting with each other face-to-face. We seem determined to give human qualities to objects and content to *treat each other as things*...[9]

Each of us has experienced what these experts are talking about. In meetings, on the street, in commuter buses and trains, in elevators, and even at home, people are staring at and fiddling with their phones and tablets, spending much more time with *connectivity* than in *contact*.

So here's the situation we're in: Our magnificent human brain empowers each of us to connect with everything and everyone around us both impersonally and personally, and strong cultural forces are pushing us in impersonal directions. We operate with only half our potential. So we're out of balance. As Sherry Turkle says, our default option is to "treat each other as things." And we do this especially with people who are culturally different from us. As a result, multicultural situations often present real challenges, and the quality of our lives suffers. We need to develop ways to resist these forces, and the first way is to set a simple goal.

chapter four

HELP MAKE YOUR COMMUNICATING AS PERSONAL AS POSSIBLE

© Syda Productions/Shutterstock.com

Beginning teachers, doctors, and managers are often advised, "Don't get too close to your students/patients/the people who report to you. You've got to maintain your distance to keep your objectivity." And yet, the people who have closely studied teaching, health care, and managing in the twenty-first century have discovered just the opposite.

For example, Ken Bain, director of the Center for Teaching Excellence at New York University, describes what he found from over fifteen years of studying teachers at over two dozen institutions in his book, *What the Best College Teachers Do.*[10] In the chapter, "How Do They Treat Their Students?" Bain describes how the best teachers "care about our students as people and as learners" (p. 139). Many echoed the instructor who said, "The most important aspect of my teaching is the relationship of trust that develops between me and my students" (p. 140). They "displayed a kind of openness" and "shared with students their secrets about learning [or] how they remembered something" (p. 141) and emphasized that "each contribution is unique" (p. 142). "The best teachers generally. . . tried to take their students seriously as human beings. . . [and] felt a bond between themselves and their students in humankind's struggles to know anything" (pp. 143, 145).

In other words, these teachers helped make their communicating with their students *as personal as possible.* "Helped make" because communication is a two-way street, and they can only control what's on their side. Their goal, though, is not to wear their heart on their sleeve or to pry into their students' private lives, but to encourage contact that is *as personal as possible.*

Physicians are getting the same advice. Since 2008, doctors from the World Medical Association, the World Organization of Family Doctors, the World Psychiatric Association, and dozens of other groups have been meeting in Geneva to lay out the principles of what they call "Person-Centered Medicine." They begin with the conviction that the most effective medical treatment focuses on what "is *unique* about each person's illness experience. . . . The benefits of scientific progress on disease and innovative treatment technologies may be squandered and hindered if they are not accompanied by. . . care that is *person centered* and relationship based."[11] They affirm the importance to clinical care of "the dialogic basis of the medical profession," and they urge physicians to make the systemic and individual changes in health care delivery that can make personal contact a regular reality.

The most influential business guru of the twentieth century encourages his readers to move in the same direction. Stephen R. Covey continually advises managers to flatten organizational hierarchies, develop meaningful relationships, and, especially, to learn to listen empathically. "Seek first to understand and then to be understood," he urges. "Find your voice and inspire others to find theirs."[12] Covey focuses squarely on "the human side of organizations," especially the danger of "treating people like things" which "insults and alienates them, depersonalizes work, and creates a low-trust, unionized, litigious cultures" (p. 16). Covey's 2011 book argues that "the most challenging walls that imprison the human mind [are] the walls between people [that] form barriers to trust, communication, and creativity."[13]

These education, medical, and management experts are all encouraging their readers and listeners to *help make their communicating as personal as possible*. I've already said what this *doesn't* mean—wearing your heart on your sleeve or prying into someone's private life. It's also obvious that sometimes you don't want your relationship to be as personal as possible. It'd be a waste of time and effort with a ticket-taker, a cafeteria-server, and most bank tellers. Sometimes you don't want personal contact because of power, safety, appropriateness, or the time you have. This is why this goal is *"as personal AS POSSIBLE."*

You don't need to start from ground zero, because, as I said, you've already done this with some members of your family, your loved ones, and some colleagues and friends. On the other hand, most of us do not do this very well with people who are culturally different from ourselves. Age, racial, ability, and gender stereotypes are snapshots of *impersonal* contact.

Set a goal to restore some balance to your life by pushing back against all the cultural forces that are moving you in *impersonal* directions. Rediscover what the *personal* powers of your brain can do for you. Benefit from the direct engagement, efficiency, clarity, excitement, comfort, and often the joy and even transformation that *personal* contact can provide.

WHAT'S AT STAKE

Today people are insulting, attacking, and even killing people they think are Muslim and some radical Muslims are doing the same things to "infidels." Police officers are shooting unarmed, young Black men. Politicians are labeling Hispanic immigrants "criminals," "rapists," and "thugs." Even some churches are preaching hatred for transgender people and same-sex couples. Depersonalization fuels this violence; and depersonalization happens when people "take in" and "give out" only the impersonal features of the people they're talking about and with. We live in a culture polluted by hostility, mistrust, and polarization, much of which is rooted in fear. Very often, we fear what we don't understand. It can be easy to hate someone you don't know personally.

Each of us can help to turn this crisis around by setting a simple goal: Resolve to enrich your life by helping to make more of your communicating *as personal as possible*, especially with people who have cultural identifiers different from your own.

chapter five

GET THESE FOUR ON THE TABLE

© JHershPhoto/Shutterstock.com

This step is the heart of it. I've said what "as personal as possible" *isn't,* and this chapter explains what it *is.*

You help make your communicating as personal as possible by using your "taking in" and "giving out" to get on the table relevant parts of four qualities that help make each of us a *person:* Our **choices,** our **emotions-spirit-personality (ESP),** our **reflections,** and our **mindfulness.** This is what Martin Luther King, Jr. meant when he told us that we can reduce our fear of each other by "communicating properly." When people put significant pieces of these four on the table between them, their communicating will be *as personal as possible,* and their contacts with people who are culturally different from themselves will go much more smoothly.

CHOICES

If you kick a soccer ball, it'll go where it's kicked, because the laws of physics determine its trajectory. If you kick a person, the result could be anything from giggles to a lawsuit. Why? Because choice intervenes between the kick and what the person does. Humans are making choices all the time, based on cultural background, family values, preferences, mood, and dozens of other influences. This means that people with cultural identifiers different from yours are likely to make choices that seem unusual or even strange to you. The ability to make different choices is one of the features that help make us human. As a result, communication that considers choices will be more personal than communication that doesn't.

You can "take in" choices by listening for and asking about the other person's "first priority," "main goal," or "true desires." Also listen for metaphors other people use, and encourage them to elaborate, because metaphors often tell you about their choices. For example, an IT manager might say, "It feels like getting this new database up and running is like cutting a trail through a jungle." You might ask, "What are the biggest trees in the jungle?" or "Who can help you make the trail?"

You can also ask a person more directly, "How did you decide to. . . ?" or "Was it easy or hard to go after. . . ?" One of the most helpful questions you can ask to "take in" choices is, "What do you want to have happen?" Avoid "What do you want?" because it'll provoke defensiveness in some people. Ask the question just the way it's worded here, and I think you'll find it can help.

"Give out" choices by explaining your main goal or top priority. Describe what you really want. In some cases, it's helpful to compare and contrast what you want with what the other person wants—"I agree that we should move in this direction, but not until closer to the election." You can also elaborate your own metaphors to make your choices clearer.

EMOTIONS-SPIRIT-PERSONALITY (ESP)

If you exhaustively measure a person's blood pressure, height, weight, body mass index, foot size, serum cholesterol level, all the way down to the electric potential in the eighth cranial nerve, you still won't know who this person is, because humans have unmeasurable parts called Emotions (feelings), a Spirit, and Personality.[14] Together, these make up ESP (not to be confused with "extra-sensory perception").

Communication is more personal when relevant emotions are on the table between conversation partners, along with other unmeasurable aspects of who they are. Again, you don't have to wear your heart on your sleeve. Comments like, "I'm excited about what the new website will do for marketing" and "I'm worried about this change in vendors" can help personalize conversations at work. "I'm not the kind of person who can change loyalties this quickly" or "That's not my strength; can we ask Sarah to pick up that part?" can do the same thing. All these are ways to "give out" relevant aspects of your ESP.

You can "take in" ESP by paying close attention to emotional indicators—extraneous actions, eyes, posture, tone of voice, breathing, etc. Does it look like he can't wait to get out of here? Does she look defeated or energized? Gently ask about what you're noticing.

You can also encourage the other person with such questions as, "What's your take on this?" "What's most exciting/encouraging/challenging about . . . ?" or "How do you feel about where we're heading?"

REFLECTIONS (THOUGHTS ABOUT THOUGHTS AND ACTIONS, QUESTIONS, RESERVATIONS)

All animals are aware of their surroundings, but as far as we know, only humans have the capacity to be aware of our awareness. This is how we *reflect*. We have second thoughts and speculate about the future. We build libraries and elaborately bury our dead. All these are evidence that humans are reflective. Cultural identifiers such as gender, age, race, and sexual identity also affect people's reflections. When reflections are on the table between conversation partners, they are another way to help make the contact more personal.

"Take in" reflections by listening for hesitations or reservations. Ask your conversation partner about his or her second thoughts. One group who facilitates dialogues on hot-button issues like immigration and abortion suggests wording one important question this way:

[
Within your thinking about (e.g., abortion), do you have some areas of uncertainty or value conflicts that you're willing to speak about? For example, can you think of a time when the values you hold dear related to this issue bumped up against other values that are also important to you, or a time when you felt yourself pulled in two directions?[15]
]

Notice how this question invites others to think back and reflect on the more complex parts of their ideas and opinions. It helps avoid the oversimplified,

"This is the way it is!" or "That's ridiculous!" ways of thinking and talking. This is exactly the kind of thing you want on the table when you're working to make your communicating *as personal as possible.*

"Give out" your own reflections by sharing your reservations and second thoughts. "I think this is right, but I'm not sure," "I have some questions about. . . ," or "I could be wrong about this." You might also share your reflections about how the opinion you hold positions you in relation to others—"I know that most people here think differently, but I really believe that. . . ." Sometimes you've noticed how your view has changed over time, and this is another kind of reflection that you might share: "I used to believe that . . . and now I'm really convinced that. . . ." All these kinds of statements can help get reflections on the table.

MINDFULNESS (BEING PRESENT)

Mindfulness means being here now. It is the opposite of living life on automatic pilot. Buddhists have been studying, teaching, and practicing mindfulness for centuries. Now health science professionals at the most prestigious universities are emphasizing the importance of mindfulness to stress relief, immune functioning, and overall well-being. As a part of your communication, mindfulness means being present to the other person and helping the other person be present to you.

On the "taking in" side, one important skill is learning to postpone your own agendas. You can't be present to the other person when you're caught up in your own distractions or planning what to say next. Learn the discipline of suspending your immediate concerns so you can focus on the other person. One specific way to do this is to repeat the other person's key words or phrases to yourself, so you stay focused on his or her priorities.

You "give out" mindfulness when you are as candid, transparent, and honest as the situation permits. I-statements help here, as they do with other parts of personal communicating. Permit yourself to be vulnerable, and take some risks: "I'd like to say more about this, but H.R. has emphasized that the information is confidential," "I know the group said that they liked the new system, but I've heard many people saying they want to go back, and I agree with them," "This is a difficult topic so can we agree to stick with it until we get it resolved?" or "This is a safe space; I'm not going to talk to anybody else about what we discuss."

CHOICES, ESP, REFLECTIONS, MINDFULNESS

As I said in Chapter 2, when you are connecting with people with the help of the *personal* parts of your brain, you're aware of the **whole** person instead of analyzing specifics such as height, hair color, gender, ethnicity, or appearance. You're also personally involved or **engaged** rather than distanced and objective; and you're noticing figurative and **metaphoric**, not just literal, features. You're "into" the other person, caught up in what's being said and done. You are experiencing what some people call "the feeling of being felt." For this time, your world is filled up with your conversation partner. The personal parts of your brain empower you to do all this.

Notice how these personal ways of connecting map onto the four features of what make us persons—choices, ESP, reflections, and mindfulness.

For example, you need to be **engaged** in order to understand another person's **choices.** In order to take in and give out choices, you need to be in a **subjective** rather than objective mindset. It's also impossible to notice the other person's **ESP** unless you're personally **engaged** with him or her. In addition, people often use **metaphors** to talk about and understand **emotions**—"It's like being shut out by the jocks in high school." "I feel like a 50-year old who's just been fired and has to try to find another job." "I feel like a kid again!" Likewise, when you hear somebody's second thoughts (**reflections**), you have to understand them **holistically**, or they'll just seem like two contradictory opinions or attitudes; and **mindfulness** is another word for being **engaged**—being-here-now with the other person.

So when you do what this chapter encourages—work to get these four features of persons on the table between you—you are engaging the *personal* parts of your brain. Doing this is the heart of helping make your communicating *as personal as possible.*

chapter six
HELP UNIQUENESSES MEET

© Pool Photograph/Corbis

To review the first four steps, in order to "properly communicate," the basic **actions** you use are "taking in" and "giving out" (Chapter 2). The **possibilities** our brain empowers us with are *impersonal* and *personal* relating (Chapter 3). The crucial **choice** is to work to make your communicating *as personal as possible* (Chapter 4). The **features to get on the table** are choices, ESP, reflections, and mindfulness (Chapter 5). This chapter explains how the **outcome** that can occur is that uniquenesses may meet, as appears to be happening for Prince Harry and the young African in the picture.

UNIQUENESS

The probability of somebody other than your identical twin having your exact DNA is almost zero; and even identical twins are individuals. This is one way of saying that uniqueness is another defining characteristic of a person. Each of us is a unique combination of culturally influenced choices, measurable and unmeasurable parts, reflections, and the ability to be mindful.

Uniqueness surfaces in communication as people mindfully take in and give out their choices, ESP, and reflections. When relevant parts of these features are present in a conversation, the people will get a sense of some of what's unique about each other. This makes uniqueness the simplest yardstick for whether and when a communication event is *as personal as possible*. A *personal* contact happens when the people involved have a sense of some of what's unique about each other.

This has happened to you many times in the past with family members and others you care about or love. If you think back, I'm sure you can recall some of these times, because they were moments that *mattered*. They may have been positive or negative, but they had impact.

One of these moments that I remember wasn't all that pleasant, but it was really important. It happened in a session my wife and I had with a counselor named

PERSONAL COMMUNICATING AND RACIAL EQUITY

Ellen, when we were trying to sort out what made our marriage stressful. Ellen asked me why I'd arrived late for the session, and I described what had happened on the way. I'd rushed to my car, realized I'd forgotten my keys, slid my briefcase under the locked car while I ran back to my office, returned with the keys, and driven off. Part way there, I discovered what I'd done, returned to the lot, and found that my briefcase was gone. I was definitely frazzled when I got to the counseling session. Ellen sympathized with me some and then gently asked me how much "dignity" I thought was in my life.

Her question struck me like a slap on the face. I was embarrassed and angry at the thought that my life might be "undignified." "What are you saying?" I snapped defensively. Ellen didn't push the idea. She just planted it and helped me think aloud about it.

Pretty soon, I began to see that she'd really hit a nail on the head. She had listened to me deeply enough in earlier sessions that she'd come to know me uniquely, in this case better than I knew myself. Her point was not that I needed to be stuffy or formal, but that I should respect myself enough to slow down, be mindful, and move through life with more grace. Ellen talked about learning a similar lesson about her own life, and she shared some of the ways dignity smoothed things for her. It felt like a talk with an older sister. Although it was painful, I experienced real contact between Ellen and an important part of who I was.

As I think back on this experience, I realize that in this conversation, part of my uniqueness met part of Ellen's. She wasn't just "a counselor" to me, and I wasn't just "a client" to her. This particular conversation could not have happened between any two people in the world other than Ellen and me. Her question about "dignity" was customized to fit me—who I was right then and where I was in my life. Her report about how dignity worked in her life gave me a window into something unique about her. Relevant choices, emotions, and reflections were on the table between us. As a result, even though there were gender, age, and ethnicity differences between us, we connected as *unique persons*.

The fact that this wasn't a pleasant encounter is important. Contact that's *as personal as possible* isn't always agreeable, fun, or supportive. Its value comes from being genuine, candid, real. This is why personal contact so often *matters*.

This kind of communicating can happen in many life arenas—online, at work, in learning situations, and in spiritual and religious contexts.[16] Most importantly for this book, it can happen when you're communicating with someone who's culturally different from you.

As the next chapter explains, multicultural situations are where uniqueness is most obvious, and sometimes most challenging. If you move through the steps that are outlined in these chapters, though, you can help create contact that is *as personal as possible*, which is what Dr. King is pointing toward.

When King said "properly communicated," I believe he meant communicated as personally as possible. When conversation partners are present to each other, when they listen for choices, feelings, and reflections, when they talk about their own relevant choices, feelings, and reflections, and when parts of their uniquenesses meet, their contact will often overcome the difficult differences they're experiencing.

HOW TO HELP UNIQUENESSES MEET

TAKING IN "Take in" uniqueness by actively listening for and asking about the other person's distinctive take on the topic. This is what Ellen did for me. Ask the other person where his or her view is the same as yours and where it's different. Probe his or her feelings and metaphors, because this is where a person's individuality often surfaces. Especially when the person is culturally different from you, ask yourself, "Who is THIS person?" In my case, how is what Ellen is saying different from anything else I've heard on this topic? How is she unlike everybody else?

Remember what it's like to really get into a piece of music? Taking in uniqueness is something like this. You *let the other person happen to you* just as you let music happen to you. In a way, you move to another's melody. You grasp, sense, feel, what sets this person apart from everybody else. The experience may be something you like or dislike, but the point is, you contact him or her as a *person*.

When it's difficult for you to get a sense of uniqueness, go back to the four qualities. Ask more about choices. Watch for and check your perceptions of emotions. Get a sense of his or her personality. Check to see that you understand what questions this person is asking about this topic. In all these efforts, work at being present to the person and making it easier for him or her to be present to you.

Giving Out This will make it easier for the person to sense your individuality. Be as candid and open as the situation permits. "Give out" some of your own uniqueness directly by summarizing relevant parts of your history or how your views are similar to and different from your conversation partner's. Do the same about the unmeasurable parts of your take on the topic. Ask questions to check whether he or she is hearing your individual viewpoint. You can also paraphrase what you hear is unique about the other and ask for verification or correction.

As I mentioned, sometimes it isn't appropriate or safe to connect personally with another person. But don't be led astray by out-of-date beliefs about management, productivity, learning, satisfaction, happiness, and even health that have encouraged people to "keep your distance," "don't get personal," and "remember your objective role in the work group/family/team." Many actual studies of real people don't support these generalizations.

chapter seven

DEALING WITH DIFFICULT DIFFERENCE

"If you are different than me, why don't we talk?" © TASS/ITAR-TASS Photo/Corbis

Pope Francis and Dr. King both understand that the best way to deal with difference is to get to know each other better. My goal in this book is to empower you to do this, to help make your communicating *as personal as possible* especially when you experience difficult difference.

Difficult difference happens when you notice a difference between one or more of your cultural identifiers and another person's race, gender, age, sexuality, ability, or religion, and the difference creates a difficulty. Some examples include:

- You're around someone of a different race and you're irritated at how loudly they are talking, or how close they're standing to you.

- A person doesn't seem to believe that you're competent, and you suspect it's because you're female, Latino, physically disabled, or Black.

- You are one of the only people in the room like you, and you notice that most people are ignoring you.

- You're passed over for a reward at work in favor of a person who's culturally different from you.

- You encounter an obvious act of discrimination that you want to respond to—a joke that someone makes at the expense of a member of the LGBTQ community, ridicule of a woman in power, or violent criticism of "those Muslims."

In situations like these, most people respond with "flight," "fight," or "freeze." For example, after a young man of color assaulted and murdered a White woman in our primarily White city, people posted anonymously online that the problem was "all those outsiders we've allowed to move in," and one challenged others to join with him in "getting rid of them." This is obviously a "fight" response. On the "flight" or "freeze" side, a Black friend of mine told me that, when he's waiting for an elevator and the door opens to reveal that there is only a single White woman in the car, he waits for the next car, because he's learned that she's likely to be afraid of him. He avoids this possibility.

The pope's invitation and Dr. King's advice offer an alternative to "fight," "flight," or "freeze." As I've said, it's hard to hate or fear others who are different from you when you know them personally. This is the connection between what's in Chapters 2 to 6 and the rest of this book. **The more you can succeed at helping make your communicating *as personal as possible*, the better you'll know the other person, the less you're likely to fear him or her, and the more effectively and productively you can deal with difficult difference.**

PRIVILEGE AND POWER

Especially in the United States, the context for everybody's efforts to deal with difficult difference is shaped by the realities of privilege and power. Since this country's inception, certain people have been able to experience more societal value than others. Most frequently, these have included men, Whites, and heterosexuals. These privileged groups have attained social entitlements, often at the expense of others. This is what is known as "systemic privilege." If you're a White, heterosexual male, you may not have expected or asked for this privilege, but *systems* give it to you anyway. Many of these systems were established far in the past, and demographic probabilities continue to populate them. These systems give power and privilege to the people in them.

All three kinds of privilege (skin color, sexuality, gender) have been abused, and skin color has especially given people advantages and disadvantages for hundreds of years. For example, at various times in the past, the racial category "White" in the United States did not include Italians, Poles, or Irish. Because of the power and privilege it would give them, "High caste Hindus" argued to be classified as White before the U.S. Supreme Court in 1919, and Japanese made the same effort in 1922. Today, many mixed-race people and light-skinned immigrants from war-torn Mideast countries struggle with the advantages and disadvantages of choosing to be classified as "White," because it can make a huge difference in their lives

Whiteness makes this kind of difference, because, in the United States, most of the power in educational, law-enforcement, finance, government, health care, manufacturing, artistic, and religious organizations is still held by White people. This power reality creates a situation in which Whites usually don't have to think of their race and their unearned privileges, whereas people of color have to cope with racial issues and challenges every day. One author calls this "the normative violence of Whiteness."[17] "Normative" means Whiteness sets most of the ground rules, and "violence" means that many of these spoken and unspoken rules hurt people who aren't White.

For example, Whites can insist that it's good to be "color-blind." "I don't even notice color," some insist, "and that's the way everybody should operate." There are at least three serious problems with this claim. First, Whites are the only people who have the luxury of believing this, because we hold most of the power. People of color are forced to be aware of the consequences of being Black, Latino/a, Native American, or Asian every day. They cannot be "color blind."

Second, people of color know that everyday realities deny the possibility of genuine color-blindness actually happening. Black men regularly hear the familiar sound of car doors locking as White drivers stopped at an intersection act to ensure their safety. The Black or Latino father and son get out of their car at a garage sale and see the White woman hosting the sale immediately move to guard the cash box. On committees or in classes the lone person of color is expected to be able to report on "how you people think" about the topic. These subtle, often unintentional actions that highlight cultural difference are called microaggressions,[18] and they happen to people of color every day.

People of color also know that most "color-blind" efforts cancel out contributions that might be made by those with distinctive cultural experiences. Research shows that diverse groups make the best decisions, and the "color blind" impetus is designed to mask or deny differences that can be very productive.

In a similar way, White politicians can argue that all U.S. citizens should "assimilate" into a "melting pot" society. Again, people of color experience acts of hatred that show them that this goal is also wildly unrealistic, and they wonder what valuable features of their cultures they would be required to give up in order to join this "assimilated" culture.

Dozens of research studies illustrate how widespread and powerful "the normative violence of Whiteness" can be. For example, several research reports show that people of all colors use and sell illegal drugs at remarkably similar rates, and yet people of color are jailed on drug charges at rates ten to fifty times greater than those of Whites.[19] A similar situation exists in the arena of employment. In 2003, when 500 identical resumes were sent out with fictitious names to help-wanted ads in Boston and Chicago, the ones with White-sounding names received 50 percent more callbacks than the ones with Black-sounding names.[20] Evidence from all life-arenas shows that, as diversity expert Verna Myers puts it in a popular TED-X talk, "We gotta get out of denial" that Whiteness is a major issue.

REPLACE GUILT WITH RESPONSE-ABILITY

When hearing this claim about privilege and power, some Whites ask, "Why do you people always play the race card? I don't condone slavery. I support civil rights. I can't change what happened before I was born." The dynamic that combines resentment from people of color and regret from well-meaning Whites commonly produces this kind of guilt—and it only makes problems worse.

The alternative is to replace guilt with response-ability. For example, if you live where snowfall is a winter reality, you don't consider yourself guilty for the most recent four to six inches of white stuff. If you're a renter or property owner, it is also up to you to clear the snow from your sidewalk. Although you had nothing to do with creating the problem, you are expected to help deal with it. This is an example of response-ability; not "fault" but the willingness and ability to *respond* to the conditions you encounter that need to be changed.

Each of us needs to understand the realities and the crushing weight of privilege and to respond effectively in our own spheres of influence. "Understanding" is how we think globally and "responding effectively" is how we act locally.

When I say "each of us," I mean both Whites and people of other ethnicities. Although White male heterosexuals clearly created and primarily sustained today's systems of power and privilege, people of varied cultures continue them. Consider, for example, the multiracial adoration of Michael Jackson and Beyonce. Both Jackson and Beyonce invested millions in becoming what mainly White standards say is attractive and sexy and people of all colors bought into this value system. The power difference is often so great that White values can shape both White and Black consciousness, often insidiously. We all have a lot to learn about Whiteness, and it works best when we learn it together, because we can be teachers and learners with each other.

WHY "RACIAL"? WHY "EQUITY"?

RACE The examples that start this chapter are not only about race; they also include sexuality, gender, age, religion, and class. So why is this book called *Personal Communicating and Racial Equity*? Social justice advocates may wonder why I'm leaving out the other kinds of discrimination, and critics could complain again about "always playing the race card."

It's true that equity won't be accomplished until all kinds of discrimination are eliminated, but I focus on race here for four reasons.

First, although the concept of "race" is, as a widely viewed PBS series demonstrated, "an illusion,"[21] it is a very powerful one. DNA evidence shows that there are more physical differences between people of "the same race" than between individuals of "different races"; but, even though racial markers can't scientifically be used to distinguish between people, we do it anyway.

Second, as I've already mentioned, race inequities create the most pressing problems in the United States at this time in our history, and the most serious of these inequities are Black/White. Between 2012 and 2015, events like the Trayvon Martin shooting (Sanford, Florida); the police killings of unarmed Blacks, including Tamir Rice (Cleveland), Akai Gurley (Brooklyn), Kajleme Powell (St. Louis), Michael Brown (Ferguson), Eric Garner (New York), McKenzie Cochran (Detroit), Wendell Allen (New Orleans), Laquan McDonald (Chicago); and perhaps most tragically, Dylann Roof's murder of nine Blacks holding a prayer meeting at Charlotte's African Methodist Episcopal Church all demonstrate that this country's main problem is still "the color line" that W.E.B. DuBois identified in 1903. A group of social justice activists insist that "Black Lives Matter," and although it's easy to respond, "All lives matter," this group's message needs to be heard, because regular news reports demonstrate that, in many cases, Black lives don't seem to matter as much as they should.

This point is vividly and disturbingly illustrated in David Pilgrim's 2015 book, *Understanding Jim Crow: Using Racist Memorabilia to Teach Tolerance and Promote Social Justice.* In 171 pages, Pilgrim shows 141 pictures of postcards, cookie jars, figurines, board games, books, sheet music, toys, fishing lures, and other everyday items that subtly insinuated cruel and violent racist stereotypes into almost every U.S. home between 1870 and 1970. Many are still for sale today. One postcard shows five black male babies with the caption, "Alligator Bait." Pilgrim's Jim Crow Museum at Ferris State University in Michigan also displays a poster of a Black baby drinking ink with the caption, "Nigger Milk," a "Bulls-Eye Bill" target with a black face in the center, a photo of a proud White man leaning against a tree where two lynched Black men hang lifelessly, and thousands of other racist artifacts. The shockingly dehumanizing messages about Blacks cunningly communicated in these artifacts have deeply distorted American hearts and minds. Harvard professor Henry Louis Gates, Jr. calls Pilgrim's book, "One of the most important contributions to the study of American History that I have ever experienced."[22]

The third reason I focus on race is that this kind of discrimination is especially difficult to repair because of its long history. This country that we love in many ways has been built, in part, on the backs of groups that have been identified as "not White" and then exploited. The scientifically invalid idea of "race" was invented several hundred years ago as a construct to put people in power hierarchies and to justify inhumane treatment of many different groups. In the United States, colonists took land from Native Americans who had no concept of land ownership, brought diseases, and, when tribes resisted, killed them. The early years of this country were marked by widespread discrimination against Irish, Italian, and Polish immigrants; Chinese railroad workers; Japanese placed in internment camps; and, from the earliest U.S. government documents, Blacks. The U.S. Constitution originally said that slaves, who were virtually all Black, would only count as a partial person (hence the 3/5th clause) for purposes of taxation and representation. For the first 200 years of U.S. history, national, state, and local laws openly discriminated against Blacks, and both legal opinions and racist social conventions reinforced these practices.

To take just one example, the 2015 "Lynching in America" report from the Equal Justice Initiative details a version of terrorism in the United States that historically reinforced racial inequality.[23] EJI researchers "documented 3959 lynchings of black people in twelve Southern states between the end of Reconstruction in 1877 and 1950. . . ." (p. 5). "Racial terror lynching was a tool used to enforce Jim Crow laws and racial segregation. . . not merely punishment of an alleged perpetrator for a crime" (p. 5). Often, lynchings were treated as community education events, and parents were encouraged to bring their children. EJI concludes, "Lynchings in the American South were not isolated hate crimes committed by rogue vigilantes. Lynching was targeted racial violence at the core of a systematic campaign of terror perpetrated in furtherance of an unjust social order" (p. 23). Unfortunately, the report shows, "The narrative of racial difference that lynching dramatized continues to haunt us" (p. 3).

The Voting Rights Act of 1965 and the Civil Rights Acts of 1964, 1968, and 1991 significantly changed what's legal, but the hearts of many U.S. citizens today are still hardened by this 400 years of legal racism. Beliefs with this much history are tough to change. Our only hope is to confront them as honestly and directly as we can.

The fourth reason to focus on race is that several groups have found that, when they make progress toward narrowing the gaps between people of different races, they also succeed in closing gaps that are economic, and those based on gender and sexuality.[24] In other words, this emphasis can have important side benefits.

EQUITY This is another important term in this book's title. The first dictionary definition of the word *equity* is, "The state, quality, or ideal of being just, impartial, and fair." Emphasizing equity can create problems, though, because *equality* and *freedom* are two of the most basic U.S. values, and when we start with a playing field that is anything but level, equity sometimes demands *unequal* remedies that threaten some people's *freedoms*. You can't level a tilted playing field by giving everybody the same help. This would just keep the field uneven. In order to move toward equity, there are times when some has to be transferred from those of us who have more to those who have less. If this sounds un-American, remember that it's the rationale behind the graduated income tax. People with more pay more, and appropriately so.

Successful programs in schools, businesses, nonprofits, and political organizations also have demonstrated that equity work can benefit all participants. Achieving equity is not a zero-sum game. When I am respectfully curious (see Chapter 8) about a culture different from my own, I don't lose or give up anything. Rather, I learn something about that culture that enriches my understanding. When I take time to listen to someone different from me, I can experience the same kind of enlightenment that often happens when I visit a foreign country: "Naps in the early afternoon! What a great idea!" "Their constant smiling masks disagreements, but it sure helps to keep the conversation going." "I can see now that an hour of tea and small talk before getting down to business can actually help the negotiation."

As I mentioned, research also shows that diverse groups make better decisions than homogeneous ones. This means that when White privilege is diminished, contributions from "Others" often enhance group outcomes.[25] So when politicians argue against multiculturalism in favor of "assimilation," they are actually putting at risk both good decision making and public learning.

In short, if you want to deal more effectively with difficult difference, it helps to acknowledge that, much of the time, these differences have to do with race and equity. Your efforts to help make your communicating as personal as possible will take place in this context. The practical work of developing an alternative option to "fight," "flight," or "freeze" emphasizes three actions that all help lead in this direction: **curiosity, humility,** and **platinum empathy.** These are the topics of the next three chapters, because each of these can help you make your communicating in situations of difficult difference *as personal as possible.*

chapter eight
CURIOSITY

© Fabian Faber/Shutterstock.com

Curiosity is the first powerful tool to use to help make your communication in situations of difficult difference *as personal as possible.*

Recently, I found myself in the middle of a dispute about whether to change the name of a multicultural nonprofit center where I volunteer. The proposal came from the local NAACP, and the name would be of a Black woman who was a tireless champion of social justice in this community all her life. Many older NAACP members knew her well, and they deeply respect her. They believe, along with everybody else in this conversation, that her legacy definitely deserves honoring. It's also clear that the center serves many cultural constituencies, and some people believe it shouldn't bear the name of a representative of any culture. Plus, some members of the woman's family believe they haven't been fully consulted about this plan. Some sponsors of the proposal want to move as rapidly as possible, because the woman's legacy is so compelling. Before deciding, we need to listen to representatives of other ethnic groups, members of the LGBTQ community, other user groups of the nonprofit, and city council people. In order to arrive at the right decision and the right timing, we have to help make our communicating as personal as possible, which starts with being systematically and thoroughly curious.

Curiosity begins with an interested, inquisitive mindset. When curious, a person wants to know or learn. The curious person wonders and asks genuine questions: "Well look at that! I wonder what's going on there?" "I sure didn't expect that! I need to figure out what's going on." Or, as Pope Francis put it, "If you are different than me, why don't we talk?"

You can mobilize curiosity to help with situations of difficult difference by focusing it first on yourself and then on others.

TAKING YOUR OWN CULTURAL INVENTORY

Being curious about yourself starts with taking your own cultural inventory. You cannot cope comfortably with difficult difference unless and until you know clearly where *you* are located culturally.

One way to do this is to use an "identity wheel." You begin with a circle representing the whole you, and you divide the circle into seven pie-shaped pieces that identify your race, gender, religion, class, ability, sexuality, and age. The size of each slice reflects your awareness of that part of your identity. If you're very aware of your race or religion, then that slice is larger than those you are less aware of, and so on.

The second step is to identify which parts of your identity help you be *advantaged*, and which make you culturally *targeted*—a possible victim of oppression—by putting an "A" or a "T" in each segment.

Each person's identity wheel changes from situation to situation, as he or she becomes more or less aware of various segments. As I write this, though, my identity wheel looks like this:

Identity Wheel

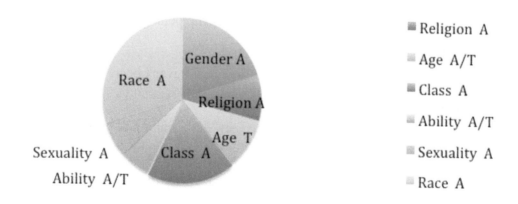

I am most aware of being White and male. My socioeconomic identity as middle class is next in significance, and then comes my age. The significance of my religion and heterosexual identity changes from situation to situation, as you'd expect, and I'm usually least aware of my disabilities, even though I am hearing-impaired enough to wear two hearing aids. They help enough to keep this element of my identity relatively out of my awareness. Importantly, all the main elements of my cultural identity help me be advantaged, except for my age, which occasionally puts me in the position of being targeted. There are times when my hearing is a disadvantage, but not very often.

As I reflect on the comments about Whiteness in Chapter 7, this curiosity about myself also leads me to notice how much White privilege I have. For example, unlike people of color, I can affirm all of these descriptions:

- I can be in the company of people of my race most of the time.

- I can be pretty sure that my neighbors will be neutral or pleasant to me.

- I can be sure that my children will be given materials in school that testify to the contributions of their race.

- I can do well in a challenging situation without being called a credit to my race.

- I am never asked to speak for all the people of my racial group.

- I can be pretty sure that, if I ask to talk to "the person in charge," I will be facing a person of my race.

- If a police officer pulls me over, I can be sure I haven't been singled out because of my race.

- I can choose blemish cover or bandages in "flesh" color and have them more or less match my skin.

- I can comfortably avoid, ignore, or minimize the impact of racism on my life.[26]

When I apply curiosity about my own cultural identifiers to the nonprofit re-naming issue, I need to be consistently and keenly aware of the privilege that comes not only from my being in a leadership position in the nonprofit but also from the facts that I'm White, male, heterosexual, and middle class, and many of the people I'm talking with are not. So each time I sit down to talk with one or more stakeholders, I need to be sure I'm making room for them to talk as freely as possible.

Another reason this curiosity step is important is, the more I am aware of the unearned privileges I enjoy, the better I can decide how to invest this privilege by being an ally to people who have less of it. I also need to remember that equity work is not a zero-sum game. Nobody has to "lose" for somebody else to "win."

Each person who wants to get better at dealing with difficult difference should inventory his or her identity and reflect on his or her privilege before going further in this project. Ideally, you'd also discuss it with both people who know you and some people who are culturally different from you. If you're a person who learns from reading, you might want to enrich this curiosity step by reading a book like Debby Irving's, *Waking Up White and Finding Myself in the Story of Race.*[27]

BEING CURIOUS ABOUT OTHERS

In a situation of difficult difference, it's also important to be curious about oth-er(s), first, because of the way curiosity displaces defensiveness. When you're in a "Well, that's interesting; I wonder what's going on?" mode, it's impossible, at the same time, to be accusing or attacking somebody. It's much easier, too, to help make your communicating as personal as possible.

Curiosity can also help bring out the best in other people. When others take an interest in who we are and the things we do, when they ask us genuine questions and behave in ways that show us they are sincerely curious about the things we care about, we light up. People appreciate being treated as "an expert."

When I texted the NAACP president and asked to meet with him so I could listen to him further, he readily agreed, and brought his vice-president with him. At one point in the conversation, the vice-president heard me accusing "you Black people of always doing this." I was surprised by his interpretation, and worked to stay curious about it, rather than being defensive. We had to stay engaged for quite a while to work through this difficult difference. We spent two hours together, and all three of us learned from the intense conversation.

The point is to respond to difficult difference first with an inquiring mindset and genuine questions rather than attacks, sarcasm, or defensiveness. Chapters 4, 5, and 6 give you specific suggestions about how to "be curious" in each discussion of the "taking in" part of communication.

Sometimes, your curiosity will be put down with another attack. Sometimes the other person will ignore you or walk away. And sometimes, especially when it's paired with humility and platinum empathy, curiosity can help lead to a genuinely fruitful conversation.

chapter nine
HUMILITY

© Kapoor Baldev/Sygma/Corbis

Humility means holding a modest opinion of your own importance like Mother Teresa in the photo. It means having a clear understanding of, and respect for, your own and the other person's point of view.

Some people think humility means being lowly or insignificant, but it actually means being well grounded, anchored in the clear realization that you are not the center of the universe. Despite what some entertainers, sports figures, and politicians seem to believe, it's not all about the individual. Each of us plays more or less important roles in the situations we inhabit, depending on what's going on and who else is around. When my children are in the room, I have some authority because I'm the dad, but in a group of singers, I'm just a person who can barely carry a tune. And even when I'm dad, I don't know even close to everything about my kids' lives. So I need to stay well grounded in my own limitations.

Cultural humility is trickier than staying well grounded in your family or at work, because most of us are pretty automatically ethnocentric. As we grow up, we develop a set of cultural commitments that are held by people like us—Asian Americans, Whites in poverty, Black activists, academics, wealthy Christians—and we uncritically accept these attitudes and behaviors as "normal." As a result, almost everybody has to work to counter the ethnocentrism that we've unconsciously inherited from our home cultures.

One huge benefit of using the identity wheel to take your own cultural inventory is that you understand *what you need to be humble about.* In my case, I need to learn to hold my Whiteness, maleness, age, heterosexuality, and my activist commitments lightly.

By "holding each cultural commitment lightly," I mean that you understand that, since not everybody is male, for example, or heterosexual, you can expect that, if you *are* male and heterosexual, some of what you value and what you believe is "normal" will not be valued or considered normal by others. When you live with this expectation, you're not surprised to find yourself around somebody who's "talking way too loudly," "behaving flamboyantly," ignoring people like

PERSONAL COMMUNICATING AND RACIAL EQUITY

you, or getting a promotion you think you deserved. And when you're not surprised—when you actually *expect* these differences—you're much less likely to respond defensively or aggressively toward them. Your response is something like, "OK, there's a clear difference between us," or maybe "OK, there's an obvious difference that I didn't expect," rather than some silent or spoken version of, "I can't believe you're doing <u>that</u>!" or "Where did that crazy/offensive/immoral idea come from?!"

Importantly, holding each element of your cultural identity lightly does not mean that you have to abandon any of them. For example, even if it was possible, a White person wouldn't have to give up his or her Whiteness to have a fruitful conversation with a person of color. The White person would just need to remember that the conversation partner doesn't enjoy as many unearned privileges. In this case, too, as the more privileged in the conversation, the White person would have to accept the responsibility to be aware and respectful of this fact.

In the conversations about the nonprofit renaming issue, I need to remember that I didn't know the woman with the legacy, and some NAACP members did. This means that I need to listen closely to the reasons for their passion. I also don't know whether the LGBTQ and Hispanic/Latino people I talk with are uncomfortable with having the center named after a Black person or, for example, whether it's most important to them that it be named after someone who's not a White, male heterosexual. Despite my privilege and my power in the organization (and my decades of being a professor), in these conversations I'm the student not the teacher.

To take another difficult example, if "Christian" is part of your cultural identity, and if your Christianity leads you to disapprove of homosexuality, what might it mean to hold your Christian identity lightly in a conversation with an assertively "out" gay or lesbian person? As soon as it becomes apparent that you're different in this way, you're likely to experience an immediate "fight, flight, or freeze" sensation. You're going to want to change the subject quickly, show them the error of their ways, or get the heck out of there. Curiosity, humility, and platinum empathy present a set of alternatives.

To operationalize humility in this case, you could start by reminding yourself that not everybody in the world is heterosexual. In fact, the most reliable estimates I've read indicate that 8 to 10 percent of the world's population is LGBTQ. So, realistically, it doesn't make sense to be surprised that you find yourself talking to someone in this population.

Second, you can remind yourself that, although you think of homosexuality as a lifestyle choice, members of the LGBTQ community and their allies believe that LGBTQ people are born with these sexual preferences. Humility means that you can listen to someone who is gay carefully enough to understand why that person might feel it's simply part of his or her makeup, like being tall or bald.

Third, you can remember that, after years of questioning, rejection, ridicule, and maybe worse, the LGBTQ person you're talking with is likely to be skeptical that a person "like you" will be able to listen with respect. From your position of heterosexual privilege, you might need to cut him or her a little slack.

Fourth, you can remember that understanding doesn't equal agreement. You can listen and learn about this person's ideas and about parts of the LGBTQ world without putting this part of your own cultural identity at risk. You don't have to defend your own sexuality or attack another.

Fifth, you can remind yourself of the advantages of diversity. It's good to be tolerant of people different from you—"Live and let live"—and it's much better to recognize how differences can strengthen groups. As I've noted, when organizations listen to the voices of their marginalized members, they adopt better policies and practices. When employees feel listened to, they are more satisfied in their job, which also reduces turnover and thus reduces expense for many businesses. So diversity is good for problem solving and it's also good for business.

I hope these examples give you a sense of what's meant by humility, the second of these three choices that I'm inviting you to develop into your default responses for situations of difficult difference.

chapter ten
PLATINUM EMPATHY

© Monkey Business Images/Shutterstock.com

Just about everybody agrees that being able to understand another person's condition from his perspective, or being able to "walk a mile in her moccasins," is a crucial interpersonal skill. This is the everyday definition of empathy.

Empathic listening is the communication practice that actualizes this psychological skill. Executive trainer and best-selling author, Steven Covey argues that the greatest challenge for the empathic listener is adopting the necessary mindset. It's the mindset of the person who, when he hears someone who disagrees with him, walks up to the person and says, "You see things differently. I need to listen to you." It's the mindset of a person with the courage and humility to reach outside his or her own frame of reference.

Covey is so convinced of the importance of empathic listening that he says he has

> ...devoted much of my life to teaching [it]. . . . I liken empathic listening to giving people 'psychological air.' . . . Like the need for air, the greatest psychological need of a human being is to be understood and valued. When you listen with empathy to another person, you give that person psychological air. Once that vital need is met, you can then focus on problem-solving.[28]

THE POTENTIAL PROBLEM

Paying close attention to others' feelings and thoughts, and listening empathically are useful interpersonal skills.

When you're in a situation of difficult difference, though, an oversimplified understanding of empathy and empathic listening can create real problems. Recently, for example, I was talking with a Black friend about his job search, and I sensed considerable impatience coming from my friend that I thought could create problems. If he acted on his impatience, I worried, he could shoot him-

PERSONAL COMMUNICATING AND RACIAL EQUITY

self in the foot with possible future employers. I was empathic enough to sense my friend's feeling of edginess, and my experience told me that this feeling could get my friend into trouble.

When I shared my concern, he explained why I really wasn't understanding him. The friend had grown up in the projects in Detroit, and never expected to live to the age of thirty. He was now thirty-four years old, and he felt a deep-seated pressure to get on with his life while he still had time. So I was doing my best to understand where he was coming from, and the differences between my cultural experience and my friend's were significant enough that what I thought was empathic understanding created distortion and misunderstanding.

The same kind of thing can happen when a person with a clear cultural identity interacts with a person who doesn't share this identity. Some friends with strong cultural identities have told me that they are driven up the wall by well-meaning majority people who are trying to be empathic and say things like, "I know just how you feel" or "The same thing happened to me." In many cases, this just flat-out can't be true. A White person can't know what it feels like to be stopped for "driving while Black," and a woman who grew up in the suburbs probably can't know what it's like to be jumped by a rival gang.

GOLD AND PLATINUM EMPATHY

The problem of ethnocentrism distorting empathy has been noticed by some people who have written about empathy's ethical anchor, the Golden Rule. "Do unto others as you would have them do unto you" is a widely accepted ethical principle that sets up the importance of, and the need for, empathy. This rule is suggested in the Torah (Leviticus XIX:18), made explicit in Matthew 7:12, and is a central part of Confucius' teachings about Kung-Shu.[29]

The potential problem is this: If you follow the Golden Rule as it's stated, your actions toward others will be based on your own preferences about how they can best treat you. When they're culturally different from you, the rule doesn't require you to consider these differences. This is what I was doing with my Black friend. I had been through enough job searches to know that impatience can hurt the candidate, and this can create problems. But I don't enter the search with my friend's life experience. My friend might learn from my caution that he ought to moderate his drive toward closure, but I also need to understand the limits of my effort to be empathic.

If we bump up the empathy standard, we can get a sense of how the other person is different from us, and how their understanding is uniquely tailored to their perspective and feelings. We can then put ourselves in their place with these differences intact, added on to ours, and subtracting from ours where necessary. So we can try to occupy their perspective as them, not us, just as we'd wish them to do toward us. (We wouldn't want them to treat us as they'd wish to be treated, but as we'd wish to be treated when they took our perspective.)[30]

This way of doing empathy would follow the rule, "Treat others the way *they'd* wish or choose." Some people call this the "Platinum Rule."[31] It might sound like it's almost the same as the Golden Rule, but the difference can be important for two reasons. The first is that applying the Platinum Rule forces you out of the ethnocentrism that is the default option for most of us. The second reason it's important is that the other person will experience a level of confirmation and respect from you that can significantly improve everything that happens next.

The only way to practice platinum empathy successfully is either to know the other person pretty well or to ask the person how he or she would like to be treated. A good prediction of their preference would have to be based on your knowledge of some track record of what they've liked in the past, perhaps acquired from a friend of theirs or your own experience with them as a friend. If you can't ask, then perhaps you're not so much treating them ethically as guessing what they'd like. Trying to put yourself in their place here would not seem like a good idea.

As Bill Puka summarizes,

> Without involving others, such role-taking is a unilateral affair, whether well-intended or otherwise. It is often paternalistic, choosing someone's best interest. The whole process is typically done by oneself, within one's self-perspective or ego, and it can be spun as one wishes, no checks involved. Fairer and more respectful alternatives would involve not only consulting others on their actual outlooks, but including them in our decision making. "Is it OK with you if...." This approach. . .is based on a different sort of mutuality, democratizing our choices and actions so that they are multilateral.[32]

As a practical matter, it's pretty easy to add the kind of "check" Puka suggests to your paraphrasing of the other person. When you want to practice platinum empathy, paraphrase by restating the other's meaning—both their main idea and some of their emotion—in your own words, and conclude your paraphrase with a perception check. You might say, "So you're mad enough about what happened that you think we ought to go straight to the police chief to complain, right?" Or, in another case, you might paraphrase with, "It sounds like you're afraid that she'll cut all of our hours if anybody complains. Does that catch what you're saying?" This will give the other person an opportunity to tell you whether you're on or off the mark. Then listen, to verify that you've heard the other person from his or her point of view, not just yours.

As you read these suggested words, you can see how curiosity, humility, and platinum empathy go together. A person wouldn't go to the trouble of really trying to understand somebody else unless he or she was practicing curiosity. Without humility, the realization that it's not all about you, it is difficult to set aside your own preferences and opinion enough to try to capture where the other person is coming from; and the perception check is what helps you avoid ethnocentric empathy and achieve platinum empathy, understanding from *the other person's* perspective.

chapter eleven

WORKING TO PUT IT TOGETHER

© Rolf Bruderer/Corbis

This book focuses on helping your communicating be as personal as possible, resisting the "normative violence of Whiteness," living gracefully in a race-conscious way, working to promote equity, and dealing with difficult difference. These are all hot-button issues, personally and socially. The equity and Whiteness topics are freighted with ugly history, and anchored in stubborn biases. They create enormous mistrust and fear. Anybody who believes these challenges can be met easily is not facing reality. The work requires commitment, persistence, sensitivity, self-control, skill, and great courage. There are no quick fixes. Progress won't happen overnight.

And you can make a positive difference if you apply what's on these pages.

As I mentioned, this book is short to make it as accessible as possible, but I think it would be irresponsible to finish without at least trying to demonstrate that what's encouraged here is not pie-in-the-sky idealism or naïve wishful thinking. The title of this chapter is "Working to Put It Together," because I want to emphasize that there are no guarantees. The content of this chapter is meant to demonstrate, though, that what's here can help.

THINK GLOBALLY

One organization dedicated to doing this kind of work is the Public Conversations Project (PCP) in Boston. This group "fosters constructive conversation where there is conflict driven by differences in identity, beliefs, and values. . . . [by helping] groups reduce stereotyping and polarization while deepening trust and collaboration and strengthening communities."

In 2012, they were asked to help Minnesota citizens make informed decisions about a same-sex marriage initiative. As you know, this issue is often every bit as emotionally charged as racial conflicts. After laying some groundwork and training facilitators, the PCP hosted fifty-five meals and conversations for over 1,500 citizens. They shaped conversations to help them be as personal as possible. They encouraged people to be curious rather than blaming or defensive. They presented facts on all sides of the issue to promote humility among participants, and, using their own frameworks and techniques, they modeled platinum empathy.

As the sponsors reported, "We were nervous there would be yelling and blow-ups but after a few conversations we realized that wasn't happening... People were treating each other humanely. . . .Our objective was to convince the people of Minnesota that we can talk about divisive issues while maintaining—or even enhancing—our relationships with each other. And I'm absolutely confident we did that."[33]

ACT LOCALLY

To take a situation closer to home, some of us at the nonprofit where I volunteer are having difficulties with a group using some of our space for their regular meetings. Their ways of problem solving are clearly different from what I expect as an older, White, heterosexual male. When they meet, they do a lot of shouting at each other and, sometimes, stomping around the room. In addition, their meetings usually begin five or ten minutes late, and they consistently run over the time we've scheduled the room. Often, several participants in the Tai Chi class scheduled next are waiting to get into the space at their appointed time. When the group finally breaks up, nobody apologizes for either the noise or the delay.

It's easy for me to evaluate the communication style and the use of time as uncivil and inconsiderate. I'm inclined just to tell them that they've got to clean up their act or meet somewhere else. But this is one of the groups we want to use our space. They're together primarily because of their ethnic identity and their passionate political commitments, and part of our mission is to be welcoming to this group.

So my first step is to go back to my identity wheel and recognize that I'm evaluating them through the race, gender, sexuality, and to some degree age identifiers that are shown there. A second step for me is to be curious, rather than blaming or defensive, about how they operate. I need to listen and learn.

I text the head of the group to tell him that I'd like to listen to him about this set of issues. We set a time and both he and another member show up. I begin by telling them the story of my first date with Becky, my wife, when she asked me, "Why did it take you a year to call me back?" and I realized, with delight, that this was a person who spoke honestly, from the heart. "I really value this kind of talk," I tell the two, "and I hope we can talk this way."

We spend over an hour in candid and thorough conversation about the situation. I learn that there are cultural differences between me and the group about how an engaged conversation looks and sounds. I learn that they interpret most yelling as commitment, and after regularly and comfortably shouting at each other, they go home friends. I learn that they haven't wanted to take our suggestion to extend their meeting time, because it's been this for decades, so members can remember it automatically.

Since they've been listened to with some humility and respect, it's easier for them to hear my concerns about the people using the room after them. The head of the group complains that he doesn't think that anybody at our nonprofit takes seriously what their group is doing. He feels disrespected. We pursue this concern and find that he has some legitimate reasons to feel that way *and* he is also reacting unfairly, based on experiences he's had that have nothing to do with us.

I commit to talking with the people responsible for what he experiences as disrespect, and he agrees to try to be less defensive and to keep his expectations reasonable. We're comfortable enough with each other that I can laugh about how shocked this "old White guy" was by their shouting and stomping. We part with a better understanding of each other, and some specific plans for next time.

This may appear to be a trivial disagreement, but it's really about some of the most important issues that can create difficult difference: race-related topics of respect, cultural identity, guilt and blame, public image. This relatively minor effort to help make our communicating as personal as possible and to approach the difficult difference with curiosity, humility, and platinum empathy produces results that make our future contacts significantly more graceful and productive. In other words, we've enhanced, in some small ways, the quality of all our lives.

It can work when you do.

ENDNOTES

1. M. Alexander, *The New Jim Crow: Mass Incarceration in the Age of Colorblindness* (rev. ed.). New York: The New Press, 2011.

2. Spiegel & Grau. New York, 2015.

3. http://okra.stanford.edu/transcription/document_images/Vol04Scans/401_May-1958_Advice%20for%20Living.pdf

4. S. Turkle, *Reclaiming Conversation, The Power of Talk in a Digital Age.* New York: Penguin, 2015 p. 21. Citing A. Przbyliski and N. Weinstein, "Can you connect with me now? How the presence of mobile communication technology influences face-to-face conversation quality," *Journal of Social and Personal Relationships,* (2012), 1–10. doi:10.1177/0265407512453827

5. G. H. Lerner, "Collectivities in action: Establishing the relevance of conjoined participation in conversation." *Text and Talk,* 13 (1993), 213–245.

6. Iaian McGilchrist, *The Master and His Emissary: The Divided Brain and the Making of the Western World.* New Haven: Yale University Press, 2009, p. 55.

7. http://www.forbes.com/sites/nextavenue/2013/11/25/the-lost-art-of-conversation-and-connection/

8. S. Turkle, *Reclaiming Conversation: The Power of Talk in a Digital Age.* New York: Penguin, 2015, p. 28.

9. S. Turkle, *Alone Together: Why We Expect More from Technology and Less from Each Other.* New York: Basic Books, 2011. Italics added.

10. K. Bain, *What the Best College Teachers Do.* Cambridge, MA: Harvard University Press, 2004.

11. J. Mezzich, J. Snaedal, C. van Weel, & I. Heath, "Toward person-centered medicine: From disease to patient to person," *Mount Sinai Journal of Medicine,* 77 (2010), 304.

12. S. R. Covey, *The 8th Habit: From Effectiveness to Greatness.* New York: Free Press, 2004, p. 26.

13. S. R. Covey, *The 3rd Alternative: Solving Life's Most Difficult Problems.* New York: Free Press, 2011, p. 91.

14. Many tests measure data related to emotions—breathing rate, sweat on your palms, pupil dilation. But these data don't capture what we feel when we get in an argument or greet someone we love.

15. M. Herzig & L. Chasin, *Fostering Dialogue Across Divides.* Watertown, MA: Public Conversations Project, 2006, p. 113.

16. J. Stewart, *U&ME: Communicating in Moments that Matter,* new and rev. ed. Chagrin Falls, OH: Taos Institute Publications, 2014.

17. C. M. Nelson, "Resisting Whiteness: Mexican American studies and rhetorical struggles for visibility," *Journal of International and Intercultural Communication, 8* (2015), 63–80.

18. D. W. Sue, C. M. Capodillupo, G. C. Torino, J. M. Bucceri, A. M. B. Holder, K. L. Nadal, & M. Esquilin, "Racial microaggressions in everyday life: Implications for clinical practice. *American Psychologist, 62* (2007), 271–286.

19. Human Rights Watch, *Punishment and Prejudice: Racial Disparities in the War on Drugs.* HR Reports. New York, 2000, p. 12.

20. http://www.nber.org/papers/w9873

21. www.pbs.org/**race**/

22. D. Pilgrim, *Understanding Jim Crow: Using Racist Memorabilia to Teach Tolerance and Promote Social Justice.* Toronto: Between the Lines Books, 2015.

23. Equal Justice Initiative, *Lynching in America: Confronting the Legacy of Racial Terror,* 2015, www.eji.org

24. G. E. Singleton & C. Linton, *Courageous Conversations About Race.* Thousand Oaks, CA: Corwin Press, 2006.

25. T. H. Cox & S. Blake, "Managing cultural diversity: Implications for organizational competitiveness," *Academy of Management Executive, 5* (1991), 45–56; K. W. Phillips, "How diversity makes us smarter," (2014), http://www.scientificamerican.com/article/how-diversity-makes-us-smarter

26. From Peggy McIntosh, "White privilege: Unpacking the invisible knapsack," https://www.deanza.edu/faculty/.../WhitePrivilege.pdf

27. Boston: Elephant Room Press, 2013.

28. S. R. Covey, *The 3rd Alternative,* p.48.

29. http://www.iep.utm.edu/goldrule/

30. Bill Puka explains this at http://www.iep.utm.edu/goldrule/

31. http://wisdomwebsite.com/the-platinum-rule-a-golden-rule-upgrade/

32. http://www.iep.utm.edu/goldrule/

33. http://www.publicconversations.org/impact-stories/same-sex-marriage-minnesota#sthash.A8oItTXz.dpuf

CPSIA information can be obtained
at www.ICGtesting.com
Printed in the USA
LVOW02s2121180816

500830LV00003B/18/P